Table of

Dedication 2

Chapter 1: Faith Was All I Had 3

Chapter 2: Faith That Walks Through Fire 7

Chapter 3: Change Your Thinking, Change Your World 11

Chapter 4: Speak What You Believe 15

Chapter 5: Faith to Move What's Been Stuck 19

Chapter 6: The God-Kind of Faith to Forgive: When Betrayal Hits Close 23

Chapter 7: Faith When It Feels Like God Is Silent 27

Chapter 8: Faith to Finish What You Started 31

Chapter 9: Faith for What You've Never Seen Before 35

Chapter 10: Faith That Fights Back 39

Chapter 11: Faith to Stand When Others Fall 43

Final Chapter: Faith That Finishes With Fire 47

Dedication

To the one who stood beside me when I almost gave up

Your quiet strength and unwavering prayers carried me farther than you'll ever know.

To every dreamer who's been knocked down but still dares to believe

This book is for you. May the God-kind of faith rise in you and never let go.

Chapter 1: Faith Was All I Had

I didn't start with much. No big bank account. No head start. No safety net. What I did have was grit and faith. Real faith. The kind you don't read about in books but wrestle with on your knees. The kind of faith that doesn't look pretty, but it holds when everything else falls apart.

I grew up in a world where hope had to be borrowed and faith was the only currency you could spend without approval. I learned early on that if I was going to survive, it would be because I believed God for things nobody else could see. I didn't know it back then, but that belief? That was the beginning of the God-kind of faith.

See, the God-kind of faith isn't just Sunday morning faith. It's not the type that shouts loud in church and quits quietly on Monday. It's the faith that keeps going when everything says stop. It's the kind of faith that shows up in the projects, in the pain, and in the

God Kind of Faith

middle of pressure. It doesn't just believe in God it believes like God.

I've had moments where all I had was a whisper from heaven and a fight in my spirit. No blueprint. No backup. Just faith. And that faith moved mountains that fear tried to build around me.

There was a time I stood on an empty lot with no money in my pocket and declared, "I'm going to build something here." People laughed. But heaven listened. And God responded. Today, that lot has homes that shelter families because I dared to believe when it made no sense.

The God-kind of faith doesn't wait for confirmation. It moves at the sound of God's voice. It steps out of boats in the middle of storms. It believes that what's invisible is more powerful than what's in front of you. And it knows that faith doesn't always make life easier it just makes it possible.

God Kind of Faith

This book isn't about theory. It's about testimony. It's about walking through fire and discovering that faith doesn't burn it refines. It's about building when you're broken, sowing when you're empty, and believing when everything in you wants to quit.

If you're looking for a life that makes sense, this book may frustrate you. But if you've ever been at the edge broke, broken, bruised, and barely holding on this is your book. Because I've been there. And I'm still here.

Not because I figured it out, but because I trusted a God who already had.

I didn't know what I was doing. I just knew Who was with me.

And that's how the God-kind of faith works. It doesn't require all the answers. It just requires one word from God and a yes from you.

So let's begin.

God Kind of Faith

Because this isn't just a story. It's a journey into faith that moves, builds, heals, and restores.

It's the kind of faith that got me here. And it's the kind that will take you there, too.

Chapter 2: Faith That Walks Through Fire

Real faith doesn't just praise God in comfort—it clings to Him in crisis. The God-kind of faith doesn't run from fire. It walks through it.

Think about Shadrach, Meshach, and Abednego in Daniel 3. These young men didn't just believe in God they believed *God*. They told King Nebuchadnezzar, "Our God is able to deliver us… but even if He doesn't, we will not bow." That's the God-kind of faith. It's not transactional. It's not based on outcomes. It's based on trust.

They were thrown into the fire not because their faith failed, but because it stood firm. And yet, they didn't burn. Why? Because the God-kind of faith brings you face-to-face with the Fourth Man in the fire. Jesus didn't

God Kind of Faith

put out the flames He joined them in it. And that's what He does for us.

I've walked through my own fires. Seasons where I couldn't see my way out. Moments when betrayal, grief, and pressure closed in. There were days I preached hope while battling hell privately. But like those three Hebrew boys, I refused to bow to fear, to bitterness, to discouragement.

The Word says in Isaiah 43:2, "When you walk through the fire, you will not be burned; the flames will not set you ablaze." God didn't say you'd avoid the fireHe said you'd survive it. The fire isn't proof that God has abandoned you. Sometimes, it's the clearest evidence that He's walking with you.

Look at Abraham. God told him to sacrifice his promise his own son. He climbed a mountain with wood, fire, and faith. Hebrews 11:19 says Abraham believed God could raise Isaac from the dead if necessary. That's the kind of faith that obeys when it doesn't make sense. That's fire-walking faith.

God Kind of Faith

Even Jesus, in Gethsemane, showed us what it means to walk in the God-kind of faith. He prayed, "Not My will, but Yours be done." That wasn't weakness. That was surrender. The God-kind of faith doesn't mean you don't feel pressure. It means you yield to purpose despite it.

Every fire you walk through will test what you believe. It will expose whether your faith is emotional or anchored. But if you stand if you trust if you worship when it hurts, you'll find that fire can't destroy what God designed.

You may feel like you're walking through a furnace right now. Maybe it's family trouble, financial strain, or internal warfare. But I came to remind you: if God brought you to it, He'll bring you through it. He didn't promise comfort. He promised His presence.

So don't quit in the fire. Don't bow to fear. Don't let the enemy tell you this is the end. The God-kind of faith declares, "Even in this I believe."

God Kind of Faith

Let the fire purify you. Let it refine your voice, your vision, and your victory.

Because when you come out you won't even smell like smoke.

That's the power of the God-kind of faith.

Chapter 3: Change Your Thinking, Change Your World

The battlefield of faith begins in the mind. Before God changes your situation, He first changes your perspective. The God-kind of faith doesn't just believe for miracles it thinks differently. It sees differently. It speaks differently. Because what's in your mind will eventually manifest in your life.

Romans 12:2 declares, "Be transformed by the renewing of your mind." Transformation isn't magic it's mental. God doesn't bless confusion. He blesses clarity. And clarity begins when your thoughts align with His Word.

Think about the twelve spies sent to explore the Promised Land in Numbers 13. Ten came back saying, "We are like grasshoppers in our own sight." But Joshua and Caleb saw the same land and said, "We are well able." What was the difference? Not the giants. Not the land.

God Kind of Faith

Their thinking. Ten saw obstacles. Two saw opportunity. Ten saw defeat. Two saw destiny. And only the two entered the land. Why? Because their mindset matched their mission.

The God-kind of faith refuses to agree with fear. It doesn't shrink back. It doesn't live under the weight of "what if." It believes, "All things are possible to him who believes" (Mark 9:23). That's not motivational talk. That's biblical truth. And until your mind is soaked in that truth, your world will stay small even if your dreams are big.

Proverbs 23:7 says, "As a man thinketh in his heart, so is he." If you think small, you'll live small. If you think defeated, you'll settle for crumbs. But when your mind is renewed by faith, you'll start expecting overflow, walking in boldness, and declaring things that only God can make happen.

I used to walk past neighborhoods and think, "That could never be me." I thought my past disqualified me from prosperity. But one day, God challenged me:

God Kind of Faith

"Why not you?" That was the shift. I started reading His Word not as history but as my inheritance. I started thinking like a lender, not a borrower. Like a builder, not a beggar. And my life began to change because my mind changed first.

Jesus taught this repeatedly. When He fed the 5,000, He didn't see lack. He saw seed. Five loaves and two fish looked like "not enough" to the disciples but Jesus lifted it, gave thanks, and fed a multitude. Why? Because faith doesn't count what you have. It believes in who God is. And once your mind embraces that truth, miracles start flowing.

The enemy's biggest attack isn't your body it's your mind. He wants you to believe that where you are is where you'll stay. That what you've done is who you are. But the Word of God breaks that lie. It says you are

chosen, royal, redeemed, more than a conqueror.

If you want to change your life, start by changing your thoughts. Fill your mind with His promises. Reject

God Kind of Faith

fear-based thinking. Rebuke lies that limit you. Because the moment your thinking shifts your whole world begins to shift.

Faith isn't just a belief system. It's a thought system. And when you start thinking God's thoughts you'll start living God's results.

The God-kind of faith teaches you this: If you change your thinking you'll change your world.

Chapter 4: Speak What You Believe

Faith that is silent is faith that is limited. The God-kind of faith doesn't just believe it speaks. It declares. It calls things that are not as though they were.

From the very beginning, God demonstrated this principle. In Genesis 1, He didn't think light He spoke it. "Let there be light," and there was light. Creation responded to His voice. Not because of volume, but because of authority. And that same authority is in you when you speak with faith.

Proverbs 18:21 reminds us, "Death and life are in the power of the tongue." What you say shapes what you see. If your words are filled with fear, doubt, and negativity, don't be surprised when your world reflects that. But when you speak life when you declare God's promises out loud you shift the atmosphere around you.

God Kind of Faith

Jesus understood this fully. When He encountered storms, He didn't panic. He spoke. "Peace, be still." And nature obeyed. When He stood outside Lazarus' tomb, He didn't plead He commanded. "Lazarus, come forth!" Faith speaks to the impossible and expects a response.

The Roman centurion in Matthew 8 understood the power of a spoken word. He told Jesus, "Just say the word, and my servant will be healed." That's the God kind of faith it doesn't need evidence. It needs a word.

And here's the truth: you have the same ability. Not to speak from emotion, but from revelation. To open your mouth and align your words with what God has already said. When you do, you activate heaven.

There were seasons in my life where I felt stuck financially, emotionally, spiritually. I thought I needed a breakthrough. But what I really needed was a new declaration. I began speaking God's Word over my life daily. I didn't feel rich but I declared provision. I didn't feel strong but I declared victory. I didn't see doors but I declared open gates. And things began to

God Kind of Faith

shift. 2 Corinthians 4:13 says, "I believed, and therefore I spoke." That's the cycle of faith. First, believe it. Then, speak it. Faith isn't just internal it's verbal. Your voice gives it release.

Ezekiel stood in a valley full of dry bones. God asked, "Can these bones live?" And then instructed him, "Prophesy to these bones." Ezekiel didn't perform a ritual. He didn't sing a song. He spoke. And as he spoke, bones rattled. Breath returned. What was dead came back to life—not through touch, but through declaration.

What dead thing in your life needs a word? What have you been thinking about that you haven't started speaking over? Start speaking life over your marriage. Declare healing over your body. Speak restoration over your children. Call forth business opportunities, peace, favor, and strength. Speak what you believe, not what you feel.

Don't wait until it looks right to speak right. Speak in faith, and your world will start to align with your words.

God Kind of Faith

This is the God-kind of faith. It believes. It speaks. And it sees.

Your miracle might be waiting on your mouth.

Chapter 5: Faith to Move What's Been Stuck

Some things in life don't move until faith gets involved. I'm talking about the stuff that's been stuck cycles, strongholds, patterns, and pain that have lingered longer than they should. The God-kind of faith doesn't just deal with the now. It confronts what's been stuck for years and says, "You can't stay here."

In John 5, Jesus approached a man at the pool of Bethesda. He had been there for 38 years stuck. Waiting for the waters to move. Waiting on the system. Waiting on someone to help. Jesus didn't entertain the excuses. He asked one question: "Do you want to be made well?" Then He said, "Rise, take up your bed and walk." And immediately, the man moved.

The God-kind of faith doesn't just wait on the right conditions it moves on the right word. That man

God Kind of Faith

didn't need a crowd. He needed courage. And when he responded in faith, what had been stuck for 38 years shifted in a moment.

I've lived this. There were moments in my life where I was tired of praying for change and not seeing movement. It felt like things were circling relationships, business, even my own thoughts. But the moment I activated faith not just in emotion, but in obedience things started to break open.

Look at the woman with the issue of blood in Mark 5. She had been bleeding for 12 years. Doctors failed. Money ran out. But she said within herself, "If I can just touch the hem of His garment, I'll be made whole." That wasn't just desperation that was divine faith. She pressed through the crowd, touched Jesus, and instantly, what had been stuck for over a decade was healed. Here's the truth: some things won't move until your faith moves first.

Paul and Silas were stuck in a prison cell in Acts 16. Chains on their feet. Doors locked. Surrounded by darkness. But they didn't wait for a key. They lifted up praise. And their worship became the earthquake that broke the chains not just for them, but for everyone around them.

Faith doesn't just move mountains it shakes prisons. Sometimes we've allowed delay to convince us that we're disqualified. But the God-kind of faith doesn't agree with delay. It speaks into it. It declares, "Now faith is the substance of things hoped for..." (Hebrews 11:1). Not next week. Not next year. *Now.*

Stuck places are spiritual battlegrounds. The enemy hopes that the longer you stay still, the more you'll settle. But when faith shows up, it says, "I wasn't created to sit here." It stirs something inside of you that says, "I'm not waiting another year for what God said I could have now."

What's been stuck in your life? Your finances? Your confidence? Your calling? Your relationships? Speak to it. Move toward it. Refuse to camp in delay.

God Kind of Faith

The same Spirit that raised Jesus from the dead lives in you (Romans 8:11). And if resurrection power is inside you, stagnation has no legal right to stay.

It's time to rise.

It's time to walk.

It's time to believe again.

This is the God-kind of faith. The faith that moves what's been stuck and never looks back.

Chapter 6: The God-Kind of Faith to Forgive: When Betrayal Hits Close

The deepest wounds don't come from strangers they come from those we trusted.

You can survive attacks from enemies. But what about betrayal from friends? Family? People you prayed for? Poured into? People who said, "I've got your back," only to stab you in it?

That kind of pain isn't just emotional. It's spiritual. And it's why you need the God-kind of faith—to forgive when it feels impossible.

Jesus knew this pain. Judas wasn't a stranger. He was a disciple. He walked with Jesus. Heard His teachings. Watched His miracles. And yet for thirty pieces of silver he kissed Jesus not in love, but in betrayal.

God Kind of Faith

But here's the power of Jesus: He never stopped loving Judas. He still washed his feet. He still gave him a seat at the table. Why? Because the God-kind of faith is strong enough to forgive even the one who caused the crucifixion.

Joseph knew betrayal too. His own brothers threw him in a pit, sold him into slavery, and lied to their father about his death. But when Joseph rose to power and saw his brothers again, he didn't seek revenge. He spoke words of grace: "You meant it for evil, but God meant it for good" (Genesis 50:20). That's the God-kind of faith. It sees pain through the lens of purpose.

It's not easy. I've had people walk away in my lowest moments. I've been lied on, misjudged, left to fight alone by those I thought were for me. And I've wrestled oh, I've wrestled with bitterness. But every time, the Spirit whispered, "Forgive." Not because they were right. Not because they apologized. But because unforgiveness is a prison and the God-kind of faith sets people free, starting with you.

God Kind of Faith

Jesus taught us in Matthew 6:14–15, "If you forgive others their sins, your heavenly Father will also forgive you. But if you do not forgive… neither will your Father forgive you." That's not a suggestion. That's a spiritual law. Forgiveness is not weakness. It's warfare. It breaks generational bitterness. It uproots spiritual poison. It releases you from what was done and it positions you for what's next.

David loved his son Absalom. But Absalom turned the people against him, plotted to steal his throne, and brought war into David's house. Yet even in death, David wept, "O Absalom, my son…" Forgiveness doesn't mean you let betrayal continue it means you release the offense so it no longer controls you.

The God-kind of faith doesn't ignore the pain. It just refuses to let the pain define you. It trusts that vengeance belongs to God (Romans 12:19), and healing belongs to you.

Let me say this to you personally: What they did hurt. It wasn't fair. And it changed something in you. But you

God Kind of Faith

don't have to stay stuck in that moment. You don't have to keep rehearsing it. You don't have to carry it anymore.

The God-kind of faith says, "I release them. I forgive them. I'm moving forward."

Why? Because your purpose is too big to be held hostage by the past.

You may not forget but you can forgive.

You may still cry but you can heal.

You may never get closure but you can walk in peace.

And that's what the God-kind of faith offers: freedom from the inside out.

Forgive them. Not because they deserve it but because you do.

Chapter 7: Faith When It Feels Like God Is Silent

There's a kind of faith you don't learn in the spotlight it's forged in the silence.

It's the faith you build when heaven feels quiet, when prayers go unanswered, and when your soul cries out, "God, where are You?" The God-kind of faith doesn't just shout when the victory comes. It trusts when there's no sign at all.

Job knew that silence. He lost everything—his wealth, his children, his health. And for a long time, God said nothing. His friends had opinions. His wife told him to give up. But Job stood in the silence and said, "Though He slay me, yet will I trust Him" (Job 13:15). That's not ordinary faith. That's the God-kind of faith.

God Kind of Faith

It's easy to believe when you're hearing clear instructions. But what about when you hear nothing? What about when you've fasted, prayed, cried and all you get is stillness?

Hannah wept year after year for a child while her rival provoked her. She went to the temple and poured out her soul. No answer. No angel. Just a priest who thought she was drunk. But she kept going. Kept praying. Kept believing. And in the silence, God was shaping a miracle.

Sometimes God is silent not because He's absent but because He's working.

When Jesus prayed in Gethsemane, He didn't hear a voice from heaven. No dove descended. He sweat drops of blood in agony. Silence. Yet He said, "Nevertheless, not My will, but Yours be done." That kind of surrender is what the God-kind of faith looks like in its purest form.

God doesn't always shout His love. Sometimes He trusts you to believe it anyway.

God Kind of Faith

There have been times in my life where I preached faith but cried in silence. Where I led others while questioning, "Lord, what about me?" But in every silent season, God was not punishing me He was purifying me. He was teaching me that real faith doesn't need applause. It just needs God.

Isaiah 40:31 says, "They that wait upon the Lord shall renew their strength…" Waiting isn't weakness. It's worship. It says, "I'll trust You when it hurts. I'll praise You in the pause. I'll believe even when You're quiet." The God-kind of faith believes God is good 9even when nothing feels good.

If you're in a season of silence, I want to remind you: silence doesn't mean abandonment. Delay is not denial. Hidden is not forgotten. God is closer than you think.

And when He does speak when the answer finally comes you'll realize the silence wasn't wasted. It was working something in you: endurance, intimacy, trust, and unshakable faith.

God Kind of Faith

Hold on. Heaven hasn't changed its mind about you.

The God-kind of faith says, "Even when I don't hear You I still believe You."

Chapter 8: Faith to Finish What You Started

Starting is easy. Finishing takes faith.

Anybody can get excited at the beginning when the vision is fresh, the crowd is cheering, and the momentum is moving. But what happens when it gets hard? When the cost is more than you expected? When people stop clapping and the progress slows down? That's where the God-kind of faith is tested not in the launch, but in the finish.

Nehemiah faced this firsthand. God gave him a vision to rebuild the broken walls of Jerusalem. He started strong. But as the work progressed, enemies rose up. They mocked him. Threatened him. Tried to distract him. But Nehemiah had the God-kind of faith. He said, "I am doing a great work, and I cannot come down" (Nehemiah 6:3). That's the mindset of a finisher. He

God Kind of Faith

didn't stop. He didn't fold. He stayed on the wall and the wall got finished in 52 days.

Finishing requires focus. The enemy won't attack you if you're not building something. But when you're close to breakthrough, close to harvest, close to completing what God called you to do—that's when hell sends its strongest resistance.

Paul said in 2 Timothy 4:7, "I have fought the good fight, I have finished the race, I have kept the faith." That's what I want on my tombstone. Not that I started well but that I finished strong. Paul didn't say it was easy. He said it was a fight. But faith gave him the strength to endure. You need that same kind of faith not just to start your business, your ministry, your marriage but to finish it with integrity and fire. The God-kind of faith doesn't retreat when it gets tough. It leans in. It believes that what God began, He is faithful to complete (Philippians 1:6).

Jesus is the ultimate finisher. On the cross, bruised, bleeding, and betrayed, He didn't quit. He didn't call down angels to rescue Him. He stayed. And in His final breath, He didn't say, "I'm finished." He said, "It is finished." There's a difference. He didn't give up. He completed the assignment.

I've had moments in my own life where quitting looked attractive. Where I wondered, "Is this worth it?" Ministry gets heavy. Leadership gets lonely. Building costs more than money it costs energy, tears, and nights where nobody sees what you're carrying.

But every time I wanted to quit, the Spirit reminded me: you didn't come this far just to come this far.

The God-kind of faith is finishing faith. It keeps building when people walk away. It keeps sowing when the harvest looks delayed. It keeps pushing when no one else understands the vision. It says, "If God started this in me then I will finish it with Him."

So, whatever God has placed in your hands finish it. Write the book. Launch the business. Raise the

God Kind of Faith

family. Preach the sermon. Fight for the marriage. Build the dream.

And when you feel like quitting, remember Jesus didn't. He finished so you could.

And now, with the God-kind of faith, so will you.

Chapter 9: Faith for What You've Never Seen Before

The God-kind of faith doesn't just believe for what's possible. It believes for what's never been seen before.

Real faith is not just about repeating what worked for someone else. It's about stepping into territory no one in your family, your circle, or your city has ever walked in and trusting that if God gave the word, He will also guide the way.

Hebrews 11:1 says, "Now faith is the substance of things hoped for, the evidence of things not seen." That means you don't need to see it to believe it. In fact, the more invisible it seems, the more room God has to show up.

Abraham had this kind of faith. God told him to leave everything familiar and go "to a land I will show you" (Genesis 12:1). No map. No directions. Just a promise.

God Kind of Faith

And Abraham went not because he had all the facts, but because he trusted the voice. The God-kind of faith isn't driven by details. It's led by obedience.

Noah had never seen rain. Yet God said, "Build an ark." People laughed. They mocked him. But Noah didn't build based on approval he built based on assignment. And when the flood came, what looked crazy became the thing that saved his family. That's what faith does. It prepares before it's popular.

Mary, a young virgin, was told she would carry the Messiah. She asked, "How can this be?" But when the angel told her, "The Holy Spirit will overshadow you," she didn't argue. She said, "Be it unto me according to your word" (Luke 1:38). That's the God-kind of faith it says yes to what doesn't make sense because it trusts the God who said it.

In my life, I've believed for things I'd never seen done before. I didn't grow up around developers or pastors or authors. But when God whispered, "You can build that,"

God Kind of Faith

"You can preach that," "You can own that," I said yes. Not because I knew how but because I knew Who.

Sometimes your biggest limitation isn't your environment it's your imagination. God says, "Behold, I do a new thing" (Isaiah 43:19). But to receive something new, you have to let go of what's been.

The God-kind of faith sees beyond statistics. It breaks cycles. It builds what hasn't existed yet. It believes for healing when the doctors have no cure. It expects doors to open where there are no hinges. It trusts that if God gave the word, then the outcome is already secured. You don't need a reference. You just need revelation. Maybe no one in your family has owned property God says you will. Maybe no one has walked in wholeness God says you can. Maybe the vision in your spirit scares you good. That means it's God-sized.

You weren't called to copy someone else's story. You were called to write one that's never been written.

And the pen in your hand is called faith.

God Kind of Faith

Let the God-kind of faith rise in you to believe beyond what eyes have seen, ears have heard, or minds have imagined.

Because what's ahead of you is greater than anything behind you.

Step into the unseen. It's already prepared.

Chapter 10: Faith That Fights Back

Faith is not passive. It's a weapon.

The God-kind of faith doesn't fold under pressure it fights. It doesn't retreat when resistance rises. It digs in, lifts its head, and says, "Not today, devil." Because real faith knows: the greater the calling, the greater the conflict.

David was just a shepherd boy when he stepped onto a battlefield against a giant named Goliath. Goliath had size. Experience. Armor. But David had something Goliath didn't a covenant. And faith in that covenant gave him courage. "You come to me with sword and spear," David said, "but I come to you in the name of the Lord" (1 Samuel 17:45). That's fighting faith. He didn't just believe God could win he *expected* victory.

God Kind of Faith

Elijah faced down hundreds of false prophets on Mount Carmel. One man against many. But he didn't back down. He built the altar. Called on the Lord. And fire fell. That's the God-kind of faith it confronts what's false with confidence in what's true.

And then there's Jesus. Right after His baptism, the Spirit led Him into the wilderness. For 40 days He fasted, and at His weakest moment, Satan showed up. But Jesus didn't debate. He didn't defend. He declared. "It is written…" Three words that shifted the atmosphere. Because the Word is not just a book it's a sword. And Jesus fought with it.

If Jesus had to fight with faith you will too.

I've had moments where life punched hard. Where grief, betrayal, exhaustion, and spiritual warfare hit all at once. And in those seasons, I had two options: curl up or fight back. I chose to fight. With prayer. With fasting. With worship. With the Word. And with relentless faith that refused to die in the dark.

God Kind of Faith

Ephesians 6:16 tells us to take up "the shield of faith, with which you will be able to quench all the fiery darts of the wicked one." Notice it doesn't say *some* darts. It says *all*. Faith is your defense and your offense. It shields your mind, your heart, your vision, your purpose.

The God-kind of faith doesn't pretend there's no battle. It just knows Who's already won it.

Some of you are in a fight right now. For your family. For your sanity. For your future. The enemy's been hitting you with fear, fatigue, and lies. But you've got weapons. And it's time to use them.

Open your mouth. Declare God's Word. Rebuke the lies. Stand your ground. Praise louder than the problem. Pray like your life depends on it{because it does

You were not called to be a victim. You were called to be more than a conqueror (Romans 8:37).

You're not losing you're learning how to fight. You're not alone heaven is backing you up.

God Kind of Faith

And you're not going under you're coming out with victory in your hands.

That's the God-kind of faith. And it's not just surviving it's fighting back.

Chapter 11: Faith to Stand When Others Fall

It's one thing to have faith when you're surrounded by other believers. It's another thing entirely to stand when others around you fall.

The God-kind of faith isn't proven in crowds. It's proven in moments of isolation when compromise looks easier, when quitting feels justified, and when it seems like everyone else has walked away from the truth.

Daniel understood what it meant to stand alone. Taken captive in Babylon, surrounded by a culture that didn't honor God, he could have blended in. He could've bowed like everyone else. But he didn't. Daniel 1:8 says, "Daniel purposed in his heart that he would not defile himself." That's the God-kind of faith. It doesn't look for approval—it lives by conviction.

God Kind of Faith

When the king's decree demanded that no one pray to any other god, Daniel still opened his window, got on his knees, and prayed. Faith made him fearless. And when he was thrown into the lion's den, God shut the mouths of the lions. Because standing for God will never leave you standing alone He always shows up.

Elijah stood on Mount Carmel, facing 450 prophets of Baal. One man against a multitude. But faith gave him fire. He didn't shrink back he called down heaven. Yet even after the victory, Elijah felt the weight of loneliness. He ran. He hid. He cried out, "I'm the only one left" (1 Kings 19:10). And God gently reminded him he wasn't alone. There were 7,000 others who hadn't bowed. Sometimes, standing makes you feel like you're the only one. But faith reminds you. you're not.

Peter stepped out of the boat in the middle of a storm not because the waves stopped, but because Jesus said, "Come." That's the God-kind of faith. It walks when others stay seated. And even when Peter sank, Jesus caught him. Why? Because standing in faith doesn't

God Kind of Faith

mean you won't stumble. It means when you do, grace will catch you.

I've lived this. I've stood when others left. I've believed when others doubted. I've stayed when walking away seemed easier. And it wasn't always glamorous. Sometimes it was lonely. But the God-kind of faith isn't rooted in people it's rooted in purpose.

Ephesians 6:13 says, "Having done all stand." Not run. Not hide. *Stand.* Stand when your name is being attacked. Stand when your heart is breaking. Stand when everyone else folds. Because when you stand by faith, heaven stands with you.

If others around you have fallen, don't let that discourage your faith. Let it deepen your dependence. You weren't built to follow the crowd. You were called to carry the cross.

The God-kind of faith says: "Though none go with me l still I will follow."

God Kind of Faith

So stand.

Stand in prayer.

Stand in purity.

Stand in boldness.

Stand in love.

And if you do fall fall forward in grace. Then get back up and keep standing.

Because the God-kind of faith never stays down. It rises. Every time.

Final Chapter: Faith That Finishes With Fire

This is the kind of faith that doesn't just carry you through it sets you ablaze.

You didn't walk through everything you've walked through to play it safe. You weren't preserved through battles, betrayal, silence, and storms just to survive. You've been built by fire for fire. And the God-kind of faith finishes with it.

Jesus didn't end His journey quietly. He endured the cross. He died. But then He got up. And when He did, He walked out with resurrection in His hands and authority in His voice. That's what faith does. It may look like defeat on Friday, but Sunday proves that faith finishes with fire.

God Kind of Faith

Paul, nearing the end of his life, wrote these words in 2 Timothy 4:7–8: "I have fought the good fight, I have finished the race, I have kept the faith." That's the legacy of the God-kind of faith not that you didn't cry, but that you didn't quit. Not that you didn't feel weak, but that you never gave up.

The early Church didn't just believe they burned. Acts 2 says the Holy Spirit came like a rushing mighty wind and tongues of fire rested on each of them. They went from hiding to preaching, from fear to fire, from waiting to walking in power.

That same Spirit lives in you.

So don't let this book just be words on a page. Let it be a call to rise. A call to build. A call to speak, believe, move, fight, forgive, and finish.

You have what it takes.

You have faith that speaks to dry bones.

You have faith that tears through roofs to get to Jesus.

God Kind of Faith

You have faith that worships in prison.

You have faith that trusts in silence.

You have faith that keeps standing when others fall. And now it's time to finish with fire.

Fan the flame.

Live bold.

Dream loud.

Walk like you're sent.

And believe like your life depends on it—because it does. This is the God-kind of faith.

Now go and live it.

This isn't faith for the faint of heart. This is the kind of faith that speaks to storms, walks through fire, and refuses to quit even when life breaks you.

God Kind of Faith

In this powerful and personal journey, I shares hard earned wisdom and spiritual truth forged in the trenches of real life. From abandonment and betrayal to bold victories in ministry and real estate, I invites you to discover the faith that never lets go the God kind of faith.

With every chapter, you'll learn how to:

- Believe when heaven is silent

- Stand when others fall

- Forgive when betrayal hits close

- Move what's been stuck for years

- Finish strong and burn with holy fire

This isn't just a book. It's a battle cry for those who know they were made for more. Whether you're a pastor, entrepreneur, dreamer, or fighter this is your invitation to rise again, believe bigger, and walk in the kind of faith that changes everything.

God Kind of Faith

It's not just about believing in God. It's about believing like Him.

Scripture Index

Genesis 12:1

Genesis 50:20

Exodus 14:13-14

1 Samuel 17:45

2 Kings 6:16

Nehemiah 6:3

Job 13:15

Psalm 23:4

Isaiah 40:31

Isaiah 43:2

God Kind of Faith

Matthew 6:14-15

Mark 5:34

Luke 1:38

Romans 8:11

Romans 12:2

2 Timothy 4:7

Hebrews 11:1

Hebrews 11:6

Made in the USA
Coppell, TX
02 March 2026

72686273R00030